SACRED READING

for Advent and Christmas
2016–2017

SACRED READING

for Advent and Christmas
2016–2017

Apostleship of Prayer

Douglas Leonard, Executive Director

Ave Maria Press   AVE   Notre Dame, Indiana

© 2016 by the Apostleship of Prayer

All rights reserved. No part of this book may be used or reproduced in any manner whatsoever, except in the case of reprints in the context of reviews, without written permission from Ave Maria Press®, Inc., P.O. Box 428, Notre Dame, IN 46556, 1-800-282-1865.

Founded in 1865, Ave Maria Press is a ministry of the United States Province of Holy Cross.

www.avemariapress.com

Paperback: ISBN-13 978-1-59471-697-3

E-book: ISBN-13 978-1-59471-698-0

Cover image © Thinkstock.

Cover and text design by David Scholtes.

Printed and bound in the United States of America.

CONTENTS

INTRODUCTION

Advent is all about waiting for Jesus Christ. The gospel readings of Advent make us mindful of three ways we await Jesus—past, present, and future. First, we remember and accompany Mary, Joseph, and the newborn Jesus. Second, we prepare for the celebration of his birth this Christmas so that the day doesn't pass us by with just meaningless words and worthless presents. Third, we anticipate the second coming of Jesus Christ, who will come in power and glory for everyone to see and establish his kingdom of peace and justice upon the earth.

Christ is born, and we follow him in exile and in those joyful early years with the Holy Family. We are blessed, but we are challenged, too, to understand the ways of God and how we personally may understand and respond to them now.

One of the ways we can better understand and respond to the Lord during this holy season of Advent is by rediscovering, along with Christians all over the world, a powerful, ancient form of prayer known as sacred reading (lectio divina). What better way to deepen one's friendship with Jesus Christ, the Word of God, than by prayerfully encountering him in the daily gospel? This book will set you on a personal prayer journey with Jesus.

Sacred Reading takes up this ancient practice of lectio divina in order to help you to engage the words of the daily gospel, guided by the Holy Spirit. As you read and pray this way, you may find—as many others have—that the Lord speaks to you in intimate and surprising ways. The reason for this is simple: as we open our hearts to Jesus, he opens his heart to us.

St. Paul prays beautifully for his readers:

> For this reason I bow my knees before the Father, from whom every family in heaven and on earth takes its name. I pray that, according to the riches of his glory, he may grant that you may be strengthened in your inner being with power through his Spirit, and that Christ may dwell in your hearts through faith, as you are being rooted and grounded in love. I pray that you may have the power to comprehend, with all the saints, what is the breadth and length and height and depth, and to know the love of Christ that surpasses knowledge, so that you may be filled with all the fullness of God. (Eph 3:14–19)

How to Use This Book

This book will set you on a personal prayer journey with Jesus from the first day of Advent through Epiphany Sunday. Each weekday reflection begins with the date, and some include a reference to the solemnity, feast, or sometimes a memorial on that day for which there is a special lectionary gospel reading. When these are indicated, the regular lectionary gospel reading for that day has been replaced with the gospel reading used to celebrate the solemnity or feast. Sunday reflections include both the date and its place in the liturgical calendar; any Sunday reading that includes a reference to a feast day rather than its place in the liturgical calendar uses the gospel reading for the feast day. For the sake of simplicity, other feast days are not cited when their gospel reading has not been used.

In prayerful reading of the daily gospels you join your prayers with those of believers all over the world. Following the readings for Advent and the Christmas season, each day you will be invited to reflect on the gospel text for the day, following six simple but profound steps:

1. Know that God is present with you and ready to converse.

At all times God is everywhere, including where you are at this very moment. The human mind is incapable of fully grasping the mystery of God, but we do know some things about God from scripture. God is the transcendent ground of all being, invisible, eternal, and infinite in power. God is love, with infinite love for you and me. God is one with and revealed through the Word, Jesus Christ, who became flesh. Through him all things were made, and by him and for him all things subsist. Jesus is the way, the truth, and the life. He says that those who know him also know his Father. Through the passion, death, and resurrection of Jesus, we are reconciled with God. If we believe in Jesus Christ, we become the sons and daughters of almighty God.

God gives us the Holy Spirit to lead us to truth and understanding. The Holy Spirit also gives us power to live obediently to the teachings of Jesus. The Holy Spirit draws us to prayer and works in us as we pray. No wonder we come into God's presence with gladness. All God's ways are good and beautiful. We can get to know God better by encountering God in the Word, Jesus himself.

The prompt prayer at the beginning of each day's reading is just that—a prompt, something to get you started. In fact, all the elements in the process of sacred reading are meant to prompt you to your own conversations with God. After reading the prompt, feel free to continue to pray in your own words: respond in your own way, pray in your own way, and hear God speaking to you personally. Your goal is to make sacred reading your own prayer time each day.

2. Read the gospel.

The entire Bible is the Word of God, but the gospels (Matthew, Mark, Luke, and John) specifically tell the Good News about Jesus Christ. Throughout the Church year, the daily gospel readings during Mass will come from all four gospels. Sacred reading concentrates on praying with the daily gospels. These readings contain the story of Jesus' life, his teachings, his works, his passion and death on the cross, his resurrection on the third day, and his ascension into heaven.

The gospels interpret Jesus' ministry for us. Much more, by the Holy Spirit, we can find in the gospels the very person of Jesus Christ. Prayerful reading of the daily gospel is an opportunity to draw close to the Lord—Father, Son, and Holy Spirit. As we pray with the gospels, we can be transformed by the grace of God—enlightened, strengthened, and moved. Seek to read the gospel with a complete openness to what God is saying to you. Many who pray with the gospel recommend rereading it several times.

3. Notice what you think
and feel as you read the gospel.

Sacred reading can involve every faculty—mind, heart, emotions, soul, spirit, sensations, imagination, and much more—though usually not all at once. Different passages touch different keys in us. Sometimes we may laugh. Sometimes we may need to stop and worship before we continue. Sometimes we will be puzzled, amazed, stung, abashed, reminded of something lovely, or reminded of something we had wanted to forget.

Seek to feel all of your emotions as you read. Apply your intellect, too. You will confront problems of context and exegesis on a daily basis. That's okay. Sometimes you may experience very little. That's okay, too. God is at work anyway. Give yourself to the gospel and take from it what is there for you each day.

Most important, notice what in particular jumps out at you, whatever it may be. It may be a word, a phrase, a character, an image, a pattern, an emotion, a sensation—some arrow to your heart. Whatever it is, pay attention to it, because the Holy Spirit is using it to accomplish something in you.

Sometimes a particular gospel repeats during the liturgical year of the Church. To pray through the same gospel even on successive days presents no problem whatsoever to your sacred reading. St. Ignatius of Loyola, founder of the Jesuits and author of *The Spiritual Exercises*, actually recommends repeated meditation on passages of scripture. Read in the Spirit, gospel passages have unlimited potential to reveal to us the truths we are ready to receive. For the receptive soul, the Word of God has boundless power to illuminate and transform the prayerful believer.

4. *Pray as you are led for yourself and others.*

Praying is just talking with God. Believe God hears you. Believe God will answer you. Believe God knows what you need even before you ask. Jesus says so in the gospel. So, your conversation with God can go far beyond asking for things. You may thank, praise, worship, rejoice, mourn, explain, question, reveal your fears, seek understanding, or ask forgiveness. Your conversation with God has no limits. God is the ideal conversationalist. God wants to spend much time with you.

Being human, we can't help being self-absorbed, but praying is not just about our own needs. We are often moved by the gospel to pray for others. Often we will remember our loved ones in prayer. Sometimes we will be led to pray for someone who has hurt us. Sometimes we are moved to pray for a class of people in need, wherever they are in the world, such as for persecuted Christians, refugees, the mentally ill, the rich, teachers, the unborn, or the lonely.

We may also pray with the universal Church by praying for the pope's prayer intentions. Those intentions are entrusted to the Apostleship of Prayer and are available through its website and its annual and monthly leaflets. You may get your own copy of this year's papal prayer intentions by contacting the Apostleship of Prayer. The Apostleship is the pope's worldwide prayer network and has more than thirty-five million members worldwide. Jesus asked us to unite in prayer, promising that the Father would grant us whatever we ask for in his name.

5. Listen to Jesus.

Jesus the Good Shepherd speaks to his own sheep, who hear his voice (see Jn 10:27). The passages in step five are words I felt impressed upon my heart as I prayed with these readings. I included them in order to help you listen for whatever it is the Lord might be saying to you.

This listening is a most wonderful time in your sacred reading prayer experience. Jesus speaks to all in the gospels, but in your sacred reading prayer experience he can now speak exclusively to you. If you can, write down what he says to you and reread his words during the day. Put all of Jesus' words to you in a folder or keep a spiritual notebook. Believers through the ages have recorded the words of Jesus to them, holy mystics and ordinary believers alike.

It takes faith to hear the voice of Jesus. This faith will grow as you practice listening. Ideally, we will learn to hear what Jesus is saying to us all day long—as we face difficult situations perhaps. Listening to the voice of Jesus is practicing the presence of God. As St. Paul said, "In him we live and move and have our being" (Acts 17:28)

St. Ignatius of Loyola called this conversation with Jesus *colloquy*. The word simply means that two or more people are talking. St. Ignatius even urges us to include the saints in our prayer conversations. We believe in the Communion of Saints. If you have a patron saint, don't be afraid to talk to him or her. In her autobiography, St. Thérèse of Lisieux (who was a member of the Apostleship of Prayer) describes how she spoke often with Mary and Joseph, as well as with Jesus.

6. *Ask God to show you how to live today.*

Pope Benedict XVI commented that sacred reading is not complete without a call to action; something in our praying leads us to do something in our day. Perhaps we find an opportunity to serve, to love, to give, to lead, or to do something good for someone else. Perhaps we find occasion to repent, to forgive, to ask forgiveness, to make amends. Open your heart to anything God might want you to do. Try to keep the conversation with God going all day long.

"Ask God to show you how to live today" is the last step of the sacred reading prayer time, but that doesn't mean you need to end it there. Keep it going. You may drift off in the presence of God, lose attention, or even fall asleep, but you can come back. God is always present, seeking to love you and to be loved. God is always seeking to lead us to green pastures. God is our strength, our rock, our ever-present help in time of trouble. God is full of mercy, ready to forgive us again and again. God sees us through very difficult times. God heals us. God gives his life to us constantly. God is our Maker, Father, Mother, Lover, Servant, Savior, and Friend. We know that from the gospel. He is an inexhaustible spring of blessing and holiness in our innermost selves. The sanctification of our souls is God's work, not our own.

As you read, ask the Holy Spirit to lead you in this process. With genuine faith, open yourself to respond to the Word and the Spirit, and your relationship with Jesus will continue to deepen and to grow just as the infant Jesus grew within the womb of the Blessed Mother. This in turn will lead you to share the love of Christ with all those you encounter—just as the

Blessed Mother draws all those who encounter her directly to her Son.

Other Resources to Help You

These Sacred Reading resources, including both the seasonal booklets and the annual prayer book, are enriched by the spirituality of the Apostleship of Prayer. Since 1844, our mission has been to encourage Catholics to pray each day for the good of the world, the Church, and the prayer intentions of the Holy Father. In particular, we encourage Christians to respond to the loving gift of Jesus Christ by making a daily offering of themselves. As we give him our hearts, we ask that he may make them like his own heart, full of love, mercy, and peace.

These booklets may be used in small groups or as a handy individual resource for those who want a special way to draw close to Christ during Advent. If you enjoy these reflections and would like to continue this prayerful reading throughout the year, pick up a copy of the *Sacred Reading* annual prayer guide at the website of the Apostleship of Prayer or avemariapress.com. These annual books offer a personal prayer experience that can be adapted to meet your particular needs. For example, some choose to continue to reflect in writing, either in the book or in a separate journal or notebook, to create a record of their spiritual journey for the entire year. Others supplement their daily reading from the book with the daily videos and other online resources available through the Apostleship of Prayer website.

For more information about the Apostleship of Prayer and about the other resources we have developed to help men and women cultivate habits of daily prayer, visit our website at apostleshipofprayer.org.

I pray that this experience may help you walk closely with God every day.

Douglas Leonard, PhD
Executive Director
Apostleship of Prayer

We Need Your Feedback!
Ave Maria Press and the Apostleship of Prayer would like to hear from you. After you've finished reading, please go to **avemariapress.com/feedback** to take a brief survey about your experience with *Sacred Reading for Advent and Christmas 2016–2017*. We'll use your input to make next year's book even better.

FIRST WEEK OF ADVENT

Today, on the First Sunday of Advent, we begin a new liturgical year; that is, *a new journey of the People of God* with Jesus Christ, our Shepherd, who guides us through history toward the fulfillment of the Kingdom of God. Therefore, this day has a special charm, it makes us experience deeply the meaning of history. We rediscover the beauty of all being on a journey: the Church, with her vocation and mission, and all humanity, peoples, civilizations, cultures, all on a journey across the paths of time.

Pope Francis
December 1, 2013

Sunday, November 27, 2016
First Sunday of Advent

Know that God is present
with you and ready to converse.

Many of us learned as children that God is everywhere. St. Augustine in his *Confessions* details his slow realization that God is wholly and infinitely present in every place at once, for God is not impersonal substance distributed through the created universe. St. Ignatius taught his followers to seek God in all things. So we turn to God's Word, knowing God is present and ready to speak to us.

When you are ready, lift your heart to God and receive God in the Word.

Read the gospel: Matthew 24:37–44.

Jesus said, "For as the days of Noah were, so will be the coming of the Son of Man. For as in those days before the flood they were eating and drinking, marrying and giving in marriage, until the day Noah entered the ark, and they knew nothing until the flood came and swept them all away, so too will be the coming of the Son of Man. Then two will be in the field; one will be taken and one will be left. Two women will be grinding meal together; one will be taken and one will be left. Keep awake therefore, for you do not know on what day your Lord is coming. But understand this: if the owner of the house had known in what part of the night the thief was coming, he would have stayed awake and would not have let his house be broken into. Therefore you also must be ready, for the Son of Man is coming at an unexpected hour."

Notice what you think and feel as you read the gospel.

Jesus warns us to be ready for his return. We are preparing to celebrate his birth in Bethlehem, preparing to receive him fully into our hearts as our redeemer, the one who makes us God's own children by his birth, death, and resurrection. We are preparing to see him in heaven, when we will know him as he knows us. We are also preparing to see him at the second coming at the end of time, when he shall judge all people. God help us to prepare well.

Pray as you are led for yourself and others.

"Jesus, come to me. I want to walk with you today and every day. I pray for all those souls you have given me to pray for, including those I love, those who need you and your saving power . . ." (Continue in your own words.)

Listen to Jesus.

My heart aches for souls who have strayed from me, who cannot believe and love. Love is long. Pray for them in my love; unite with me, beloved. What else is Jesus saying to you?

Ask God to show you how to live today.

"Lord, make it easy for me to mention your holy name and to give you the glory for your saving love for me. I praise you and thank you, marvelous Lord. Amen."

Monday, November 28, 2016

Know that God is present
with you and ready to converse.

"Jesus offers salvation to all. He is with me now, ready
to do his work in my soul if I let him."

Read the gospel: Matthew 8:5–11.

When Jesus entered Capernaum, a centurion came
to him, appealing to him and saying, "Lord, my servant is lying at home paralyzed, in terrible distress."
And he said to him, "I will come and cure him." The
centurion answered, "Lord, I am not worthy to have
you come under my roof; but only speak the word,
and my servant will be healed. For I also am a man
under authority, with soldiers under me; and I say to
one, 'Go,' and he goes, and to another, 'Come,' and he
comes, and to my slave, 'Do this,' and the slave does
it." When Jesus heard him, he was amazed and said
to those who followed him, "Truly I tell you, in no one
in Israel have I found such faith. I tell you, many will
come from east and west and will eat with Abraham
and Isaac and Jacob in the kingdom of heaven."

Notice what you think
and feel as you read the gospel.

The good centurion has great faith. He also loves his
servant who lies at home paralyzed and suffering. He
understands the authority of the Lord to heal. Most
touching, the centurion understands his own unwor-
thiness. Jesus is moved by this man and holds him up
as an example to us.

Pray as you are led for yourself and others.

"God, you welcome strangers and sinners into your kingdom. You welcome me. I love you and pray now for people I know who need your healing . . ." (Continue in your own words.)

Listen to Jesus.

You have faith, child. Apply it in prayer for those who come to your mind. This is how you may join with me every day to spread the kingdom of God to those in need. What else is Jesus saying to you?

Ask God to show you how to live today.

"Lord, you are great, and I am so small. But if you are with me nothing shall be impossible. Let God's holy will be done on earth as it is in heaven. Amen."

Tuesday, November 29, 2016

**Know that God is present
with you and ready to converse.**

"Your disciples were blessed to see you, Lord. I am your disciple, too. Let me see you here and now."

Read the gospel: Luke 10:21–24.

At that same hour Jesus rejoiced in the Holy Spirit and said, "I thank you, Father, Lord of heaven and earth, because you have hidden these things from the wise and the intelligent and have revealed them to infants; yes, Father, for such was your gracious will. All things have been handed over to me by my Father; and no one knows who the Son is except the Father, or who

the Father is except the Son and anyone to whom the
Son chooses to reveal him."

Then turning to the disciples, Jesus said to them
privately, "Blessed are the eyes that see what you see!
For I tell you that many prophets and kings desired to
see what you see, but did not see it, and to hear what
you hear, but did not hear it."

Notice what you think and feel as you read the gospel.

Jesus prays aloud, rejoicing in the Spirit, blessing his
Father for the ways God chooses to reveal the Son to
people. He tells his disciples how blessed they are to
have seen him, for they are not prophets and kings, nor
the wise and the intelligent.

Pray as you are led for yourself and others.

"Lord, my election to your kingdom is your election.
I depend entirely upon you . . ." (Continue in your
own words.)

Listen to Jesus.

*My child, pray too for others who do not yet know me. God
wills that all may come.* What else is Jesus saying to you?

Ask God to show you how to live today.

"Lord, give me humility to trust your working in my
life and the lives of those I pray for. Give me awareness
of my blessedness in knowing you. Amen."

Wednesday, November 30, 2016
Saint Andrew, Apostle

Know that God is present
with you and ready to converse.

"Lord, you call me to follow you. Let me immediately obey your call."

Read the gospel: Matthew 4:18–22.

As Jesus walked by the Sea of Galilee, he saw two brothers, Simon, who is called Peter, and Andrew his brother, casting a net into the lake—for they were fishermen. And he said to them, "Follow me, and I will make you fish for people." Immediately they left their nets and followed him. As he went from there, he saw two other brothers, James son of Zebedee and his brother John, in the boat with their father Zebedee, mending their nets, and he called them. Immediately they left the boat and their father, and followed him.

Notice what you think
and feel as you read the gospel.

Jesus doesn't spend time getting to know those whom he calls to be his followers because he already knows them. Besides, he knows they will be changed men by the power of his blood on Calvary, his resurrection, and the coming of the Holy Spirit upon them.

Pray as you are led for yourself and others.

"I will to follow you, Jesus, in every area of my life, for I believe your teaching and your words of salvation . . ." (Continue in your own words.)

Listen to Jesus.

I give you grace to live for me today, dear disciple, for you come to me with your heart. What else is Jesus saying to you?

Ask God to show you how to live today.

"Reveal to me, Lord, the parts of me and my life that I try to hide or withhold from you, so with your help I can turn them over to you. Amen."

Thursday, December 1, 2016

**Know that God is present
with you and ready to converse.**

"Lord, give me grace to hear your words and act on them."

Read the gospel: Matthew 7:21, 24–27.

Jesus said to his disciples, "Not everyone who says to me, 'Lord, Lord,' will enter the kingdom of heaven, but only one who does the will of my Father in heaven. . . . Everyone then who hears these words of mine and acts on them will be like a wise man who built his house on rock. The rain fell, the floods came, and the winds blew and beat on that house, but it did not fall, because it had been founded on rock. And everyone who hears these words of mine and does not act on them will be like a foolish man who built his house on sand. The rain fell, and the floods came, and the winds blew and beat against that house, and it fell—and great was its fall!"

Notice what you think
and feel as you read the gospel.

Jesus says that not what we say but what we do in
response to the Word of God is the ticket into the kingdom of heaven. If we do the will of the Father, we have
wisely built our house on a rock.

Pray as you are led for yourself and others.

"Jesus, be my rock. I offer myself to do the Father's
will. I offer myself in the service of you and others . . ."
(Continue in your own words.)

Listen to Jesus.

*My Father's will is all around you, beloved. Find God in all
your circumstances; look for God in all your choices.* What
else is Jesus saying to you?

Ask God to show you how to live today.

"Lord, give me eyes to see today. I seek you. I seek to
do your will. Amen."

Friday, December 2, 2016

Know that God is present
with you and ready to converse.

"Lord, let me see and believe in your power in my life.
Teach me by your Word today."

Read the gospel: Matthew 9:27–31.

As Jesus went on from there, two blind men followed
him, crying loudly, "Have mercy on us, Son of David!"
When he entered the house, the blind men came to
him; and Jesus said to them, "Do you believe that I

am able to do this?" They said to him, "Yes, Lord."
Then he touched their eyes and said, "According to
your faith let it be done to you." And their eyes were
opened. Then Jesus sternly ordered them, "See that no
one knows of this." But they went away and spread the
news about him throughout that district.

Notice what you think
and feel as you read the gospel.

The blind men want to be healed, but Jesus questions
their faith. When he touches them, he says "according
to your faith let it be done to you." They are healed.

Pray as you are led for yourself and others.

"Lord, I ask for faith to be healed in my own body,
mind, and soul. Give me faith that pleases you . . ."
(Continue in your own words.)

Listen to Jesus.

*Faith is action obeying God, dear servant. I grant you what
you ask. I love you.* What else is Jesus saying to you?

Ask God to show you how to live today.

"Open my eyes to every little way I may obey God and
serve my neighbor. Let me act in the power of the faith,
hope, and love you give me. Thank you, Lord. Amen."

Saturday, December 3, 2016

Know that God is present
with you and ready to converse.

You are here to command me, Lord, for I am your servant. Let your servant listen to your Word now.

Read the gospel: Matthew 9:35–10:1, 5a, 6–8.

Then Jesus went about all the cities and villages, teaching in their synagogues, and proclaiming the good news of the kingdom, and curing every disease and every sickness. When he saw the crowds, he had compassion for them, because they were harassed and helpless, like sheep without a shepherd. Then he said to his disciples, "The harvest is plentiful, but the laborers are few; therefore ask the Lord of the harvest to send out laborers into his harvest."

Then Jesus summoned his twelve disciples and gave them authority over unclean spirits, to cast them out, and to cure every disease and every sickness. . . .

These twelve Jesus sent out with the following instructions: "Go . . . to the lost sheep of the house of Israel. As you go, proclaim the good news, 'The kingdom of heaven has come near.' Cure the sick, raise the dead, cleanse the lepers, cast out demons. You received without payment; give without payment."

**Notice what you think
and feel as you read the gospel.**

Jesus says God seeks laborers for the great harvest of souls. We are to pray for more laborers. To those who do labor for the harvest, Jesus gives power to serve in every way he wills. We received without payment and so should we give, knowing that Jesus will give us what we need for this work.

Pray as you are led for yourself and others.

"I pray for laborers to go into God's harvest, Lord. Give them and me a great and generous spirit to serve others . . ." (Continue in your own words.)

Listen to Jesus.

Your prayers are answered. I give you power to serve. What
else is Jesus saying to you?

Ask God to show you how to live today.

"Give me discernment, dear Jesus, to recognize the
little actions I can make to serve you as well as guid-
ance to act upon opportunities to serve you in larger
ways. Amen."

SECOND WEEK OF ADVENT

John the Baptist is described as "the voice of one crying in the wilderness: Prepare the way for the Lord, make his paths straight" (Lk 3:4). The voice proclaims the word, but in this case the Word of God comes first, since the word of God came to John, the son of Zechariah, in the wilderness (cf. Lk 3:2). He therefore plays an important role but always in terms of Christ. St. Augustine comments: "John is the voice, but the Lord is the Word who was in the beginning (cf. Jn 1:1). John is the voice that lasts for a time; from the beginning Christ is the Word who lives forever. Take away the word, the meaning, and what is the voice? Where there is no understanding, there is only a meaningless sound. The voice without the word strikes the ear but does not build up the heart" (*In ev. Johannis tractatus* 293, 3: pl 38, 1328).

Pope Benedict XVI
December 9, 2012

Sunday, December 4, 2016
Second Sunday of Advent

Know that God is present
with you and ready to converse.

The Word of God is Truth, but we must hear that truth in the Spirit of the ones who wrote the scriptures as St. Peter says in his epistles. We should know, Peter continues, that no scripture is of purely private interpretation. The Church has the final word in interpretation of the Word. Today the images in the gospels are both beautiful and frightening.

"Lord, sometimes your Word is gentle, sometimes it is harsh. Let me be open to all and come to true understanding and repentance."

Read the gospel: Matthew 3:1–12.

In those days John the Baptist appeared in the wilderness of Judea, proclaiming, "Repent, for the kingdom of heaven has come near." This is the one of whom the prophet Isaiah spoke when he said,

"The voice of one crying out in the wilderness:
'Prepare the way of the Lord,
    make his paths straight.'"

Now John wore clothing of camel's hair with a leather belt around his waist, and his food was locusts and wild honey. Then the people of Jerusalem and all Judea were going out to him, and all the region along the Jordan, and they were baptized by him in the river Jordan, confessing their sins.

But when he saw many Pharisees and Sadducees coming for baptism, he said to them, "You brood of vipers! Who warned you to flee from the wrath to come? Bear fruit worthy of repentance. Do not presume to say to yourselves, 'We have Abraham as our ancestor'; for I tell you, God is able from these stones to raise up children to Abraham. Even now the axe is lying at the root of the trees; every tree therefore that does not bear good fruit is cut down and thrown into the fire.

"I baptize you with water for repentance, but one who is more powerful than I is coming after me; I am not worthy to carry his sandals. He will baptize you with the Holy Spirit and fire. His winnowing fork is in his hand, and he will clear his threshing-floor and will gather his wheat into the granary; but the chaff he will burn with unquenchable fire."

Notice what you think and feel as you read the gospel.

John the Baptist, a man of rough appearance, preaches to the people in the wilderness, baptizing those who repent in the Jordan. But he calls the professed religious of his day "vipers," warning them of destruction because they do not bear good fruit. Then he prophesizes about the coming Messiah, who will baptize with the Holy Spirit and fire, as Isaiah had said.

Pray as you are led for yourself and others.

"John had a mission. He spoke your truth. He spoke of you, my Jesus. Let me be as committed and as true as John in your service . . ." (Continue in your own words.)

Listen to Jesus.
I am gathering you into the granary. I wash away your sins so you may bear good fruit. Stay close to me, beloved servant. What else is Jesus saying to you?

Ask God to show you how to live today.
"I praise and adore you, my Lord, my Savior. Baptize me with your Holy Spirit that I may have power to serve. Amen."

Monday, December 5, 2016

**Know that God is present
with you and ready to converse.**
"Lord, I bow to your authority. By your Word you have power to forgive sins and to heal."

Read the gospel: Luke 5:17–26.
One day, while Jesus was teaching, Pharisees and teachers of the law were sitting nearby (they had come from every village of Galilee and Judea and from Jerusalem); and the power of the Lord was with him to heal. Just then some men came, carrying a paralyzed man on a bed. They were trying to bring him in and lay him before Jesus; but finding no way to bring him in because of the crowd, they went up on the roof and let him down with his bed through the tiles into the middle of the crowd in front of Jesus. When he saw their faith, he said, "Friend, your sins are forgiven you." Then the scribes and the Pharisees began to question, "Who is this who is speaking blasphemies? Who can forgive sins but God alone?" When Jesus perceived their questionings, he answered them, "Why do you raise such questions in your hearts? Which is easier, to

say, 'Your sins are forgiven you,' or to say, 'Stand up and walk'? But so that you may know that the Son of Man has authority on earth to forgive sins"—he said to the one who was paralyzed—"I say to you, stand up and take your bed and go to your home." Immediately he stood up before them, took what he had been lying on, and went to his home, glorifying God. Amazement seized all of them, and they glorified God and were filled with awe, saying, "We have seen strange things today."

Notice what you think and feel as you read the gospel.

That day the people see great things—the paralyzed man on a bed; the crowd; the letting him down, bed and all, through the roof right in front of Jesus; Jesus forgiving him; the scribes and Pharisees questioning his authority; Jesus asserting his authority; and the healing of the paralytic, who takes up his bed and goes home, glorifying God. Then all of them, filled with awe, glorify God.

Pray as you are led for yourself and others.

"Lord, let me appear before you now, for I need your forgiveness and healing. You can make me well and make me whole . . ." (Continue in your own words.)

Listen to Jesus.

I do as you ask, my child. Strive to sin no more. What else is Jesus saying to you?

Ask God to show you how to live today.

"Jesus, I know that you are still working wonders today. Let me recognize them and glorify you. Amen."

Tuesday, December 6, 2016

**Know that God is present
with you and ready to converse.**

"Word of God, Jesus, let any part of me that has gone astray return to you."

Read the gospel: Matthew 18:12–14.

Jesus asked his disciples, "What do you think? If a shepherd has a hundred sheep, and one of them has gone astray, does he not leave the ninety-nine on the mountains and go in search of the one that went astray? And if he finds it, truly I tell you, he rejoices over it more than over the ninety-nine that never went astray. So it is not the will of your Father in heaven that one of these little ones should be lost."

Notice what you think and feel as you read the gospel.

This little parable speaks of the love of the shepherd for his sheep, emphasizing his concern for the lost sheep and his joy in finding and returning the lost sheep to the fold. So the Father wills that not one of the sheep, "these little ones," be lost.

Pray as you are led for yourself and others.

"Loving Shepherd, find me. I long to make you happy by being found, redeemed, and returned to the fold. I pray for all the lost sheep . . ." (Continue in your own words.)

Listen to Jesus.

The love of God is endless, little one. God seeks the lost, night and day until the end of the age. What else is Jesus saying to you?

Ask God to show you how to live today.

"What can I do to help find your sheep, Lord? I offer myself to do whatever you have for me. Amen."

Wednesday, December 7, 2016

Know that God is present with you and ready to converse.

"Make my heart like your own, Jesus, so that I can glorify you with my life."

Read the gospel: Matthew 11:28–30.

Jesus said, "Come to me, all you that are weary and are carrying heavy burdens, and I will give you rest. Take my yoke upon you, and learn from me; for I am gentle and humble in heart, and you will find rest for your souls. For my yoke is easy, and my burden is light."

Notice what you think and feel as you read the gospel.

Jesus asks for a great commitment from those who would follow him. As we learn from the one who is gentle and humble of heart, he promises rest for our souls. He declares his yoke easy, his burden light.

Pray as you are led for yourself and others.

"Jesus, you ask us to take up our cross daily, lose our lives, and follow you. Yet you offer unimaginable

rewards, even eternal life . . ." (Continue in your own
words.)

Listen to Jesus.
*All my promises to you are true, beloved. Join your heart to
mine.* What else is Jesus saying to you?

Ask God to show you how to live today.
"I give myself to you, Jesus. Let me learn from you the
way of love. Amen."

Thursday, December 8, 2016
Immaculate Conception
of the Blessed Virgin Mary

**Know that God is present
with you and ready to converse.**
"Open my heart to the Blessed Virgin Mary, the Mother
of God."

Read the gospel: Luke 1:26–38.
In the sixth month the angel Gabriel was sent by
God to a town in Galilee called Nazareth, to a virgin
engaged to a man whose name was Joseph, of the
house of David. The virgin's name was Mary. And he
came to her and said, "Greetings, favored one! The
Lord is with you." But she was much perplexed by his
words and pondered what sort of greeting this might
be. The angel said to her, "Do not be afraid, Mary, for
you have found favor with God. And now, you will
conceive in your womb and bear a son, and you will
name him Jesus. He will be great, and will be called

the Son of the Most High, and the Lord God will give to him the throne of his ancestor David. He will reign over the house of Jacob for ever, and of his kingdom there will be no end." Mary said to the angel, "How can this be, since I am a virgin?" The angel said to her, "The Holy Spirit will come upon you, and the power of the Most High will overshadow you; therefore the child to be born will be holy; he will be called Son of God. And now, your relative Elizabeth in her old age has also conceived a son; and this is the sixth month for her who was said to be barren. For nothing will be impossible with God." Then Mary said, "Here am I, the servant of the Lord; let it be with me according to your word." Then the angel departed from her.

Notice what you think and feel as you read the gospel.

Mary is perplexed by the angel's greeting; she wonders how she, a virgin, can bear a son, yet she gives herself fully to serve the Lord as the angel has announced to her. How she must have wondered at the glorious ways of God!

Pray as you are led for yourself and others.

"I honor your mother, Jesus. I, too, resolve to serve you as you will, no matter how I may struggle sometimes to understand your ways . . ." (Continue in your own words.)

Listen to Jesus.

I am being born in you, too, my servant. I am your hope, your salvation. What else is Jesus saying to you?

Ask God to show you how to live today.

"Be with me today, Jesus, washing me, helping me to love others and glorify you. Blessed Virgin Mary, pray for me now and at the hour of my death. Amen."

Friday, December 9, 2016

**Know that God is present
with you and ready to converse.**

"Loving God Almighty, you are strong to save, yet the human heart resists you. Let me hear you now in your Word."

Read the gospel: Matthew 11:16–19.

Jesus said, "But to what will I compare this generation? It is like children sitting in the market-places and calling to one another,

> 'We played the flute for you, and you did not dance;
> we wailed, and you did not mourn.'

For John came neither eating nor drinking, and they say, 'He has a demon'; the Son of Man came eating and drinking, and they say, 'Look, a glutton and a drunkard, a friend of tax-collectors and sinners!' Yet wisdom is vindicated by her deeds."

**Notice what you think
and feel as you read the gospel.**

God seeks people in many, many ways that they may come to him and inherit eternal life. However, Jesus says that nothing seems to work with some people for they resist the love of God and God's servants no matter what.

Pray as you are led for yourself and others.

"Lord, break down resistance to you in me and in those you have given me to care for. We need you . . ." (Continue in your own words.)

Listen to Jesus.

My child, I am always ready to receive the seeker or the penitent. I do not stop reaching out to them. What else is Jesus saying to you?

Ask God to show you how to live today.

"Dear Trinity of love and power, I give myself to you and to your service today. Show me ways to love and give me power to do it in your name. Amen."

Saturday, December 10, 2016

**Know that God is present
with you and ready to converse.**

"Lord, thank you for being with me here and now. Teach me by your Word."

Read the gospel: Matthew 17:9–13.

As they were coming down the mountain, Jesus ordered them, "Tell no one about the vision until after the Son of Man has been raised from the dead." And the disciples asked him, "Why, then, do the scribes say that Elijah must come first?" He replied, "Elijah is indeed coming and will restore all things; but I tell you that Elijah has already come, and they did not recognize him, but they did to him whatever they pleased. So also the Son of Man is about to suffer at

their hands." Then the disciples understood that he
was speaking to them about John the Baptist.

Notice what you think
and feel as you read the gospel.

It's almost funny that the disciples seem not to hear
Jesus say that he will be raised from the dead. Nor do
they react when he predicts that he, too, is to suffer
at the hands of men. They do finally understand that
when he explained to them about Elijah he was speaking to them about John the Baptist.

Pray as you are led for yourself and others.

"Human understanding can be so dark, Lord. Your
ways are not our ways, and you are so infinitely great
and good. Give us your Spirit to understand and do as
you will . . ." (Continue in your own words.)

Listen to Jesus.

*You need only me, beloved servant, for I am the Truth and
the Way to Life. Let us be lovers.* What else is Jesus saying
to you?

Ask God to show you how to live today.

"Lord, help me to love you with all my heart, all my
soul, all my mind, and all my strength today. Amen."

THIRD WEEK OF ADVENT

Today is the Third Sunday of Advent, which is called *Gaudete* Sunday; that is, the Sunday of joy. In the Liturgy the invitation rings out several times to rejoice, why? Because the Lord is near. Christmas is near. The Christian message is called the "Gospel"; i.e., "good news," an announcement of joy for all people; the Church is not a haven for sad people, the Church is a joyful home! And those who are sad find joy in her, they find in her true joy!

Pope Francis
December 15, 2013

Sunday, December 11, 2016
Third Sunday of Advent

**Know that God is present
with you and ready to converse.**

The Word of God came by the words of the prophets, the many who wrote under the influence of God's Spirit, as St. Peter puts it in his epistle. The prophets speak of the coming of the Messiah. They also speak of the one who would come before the Messiah to make straight the way of the Lord. That's John the Baptist, greater than the prophets before him.

"Teacher, Son of God and son of man, open my eyes and heart to your Word."

Read the gospel: Matthew 11:2–11.

When John heard in prison what the Messiah was doing, he sent word by his disciples and said to Jesus, "Are you the one who is to come, or are we to wait for another?" Jesus answered them, "Go and tell John what you hear and see: the blind receive their sight, the lame walk, the lepers are cleansed, the deaf hear, the dead are raised, and the poor have good news brought to them. And blessed is anyone who takes no offence at me." As they went away, Jesus began to speak to the crowds about John: "What did you go out into the wilderness to look at? A reed shaken by the wind? What then did you go out to see? Someone dressed in soft robes? Look, those who wear soft robes are in royal palaces. What then did you go out to see? A prophet? Yes, I tell you, and more than a prophet. This is the one about whom it is written,

'See, I am sending my messenger ahead of you,
who will prepare your way before you.'

Truly I tell you, among those born of women no one
has arisen greater than John the Baptist; yet the least in
the kingdom of heaven is greater than he."

Notice what you think
and feel as you read the gospel.

Jesus speaks like a poet about John the Baptist, the one
with the great calling to prepare the way of the Lord.
Yet he ends this passage with the assertion that the
least in the kingdom of heaven is greater than John.
Jesus' way is riddled with paradox.

Pray as you are led for yourself and others.

"Lord, teach me how to embrace your paradoxes and
trust you alone. . ." (Continue in your own words.)

Listen to Jesus.

*The wisdom of God is beyond you, my dear. Seek God's glory
today.* What else is Jesus saying to you?

Ask God to show you how to live today.

"You take dust and ashes and raise them to eternal life
in your kingdom. Glory be to the Father, the Son, and
the Holy Spirit forever. Amen."

Monday, December 12, 2016

Know that God is present
with you and ready to converse.

"All power in heaven and earth is yours, Lord. I bow
to your glory."

Read the gospel: Matthew 21:23–27.

When he entered the temple, the chief priests and the elders of the people came to him as he was teaching, and said, "By what authority are you doing these things, and who gave you this authority?" Jesus said to them, "I will also ask you one question; if you tell me the answer, then I will also tell you by what authority I do these things. Did the baptism of John come from heaven, or was it of human origin?" And they argued with one another, "If we say, 'From heaven,' he will say to us, 'Why then did you not believe him?' But if we say, 'Of human origin,' we are afraid of the crowd; for all regard John as a prophet." So they answered Jesus, "We do not know." And he said to them, "Neither will I tell you by what authority I am doing these things."

Notice what you think and feel as you read the gospel.

Jesus faced constant opposition from the religious people of his day. They try to trap him with a question about his authority, but he turns the tables on them. They are not interested in the truth, and their fear of the crowd means they will not answer Jesus' question, so Jesus does not answer theirs.

Pray as you are led for yourself and others.

"Lord, I know you are the Holy One of God. I give you all authority over my life—and the lives of those you have given me to care for . . ." (Continue in your own words.)

Listen to Jesus.

Losing your life to abide in my life—that is your journey. I receive you with joy, beloved servant. What else is Jesus saying to you?

Ask God to show you how to live today.

"I need you every hour, Lord. Let me be aware of you in my life very often. Thank you! Amen."

Tuesday, December 13, 2016

Know that God is present with you and ready to converse.

"The Word of God is sometimes blunt against those who resist its truth. I open myself to all it has for me."

Read the gospel: Matthew 21:28–32.

Jesus asked, "What do you think? A man had two sons; he went to the first and said, 'Son, go and work in the vineyard today.' He answered, 'I will not'; but later he changed his mind and went. The father went to the second and said the same; and he answered, 'I go, sir'; but he did not go. Which of the two did the will of his father?" The chief priests and elders of the people said, "The first." Jesus said to them, "Truly I tell you, the tax-collectors and the prostitutes are going into the kingdom of God ahead of you. For John came to you in the way of righteousness and you did not believe him, but the tax-collectors and the prostitutes believed him; and even after you saw it, you did not change your minds and believe him."

Notice what you think
and feel as you read the gospel.

Jesus' parable of the two sons illustrates that it is not what we say but what we do that counts before God. Those who repent go into the kingdom of God ahead of those who cling to their own righteousness.

Pray as you are led for yourself and others.

"Teach me obedience like yours, Jesus, even to the end. I long to go into your kingdom with those I love and those I pray for . . ." (Continue in your own words.)

Listen to Jesus.

Your journey shall be short, my beloved, and the kingdom of heaven stretches out before you forever. Rejoice today. What else is Jesus saying to you?

Ask God to show you how to live today.

"Let me count my blessings all day long. Let me rejoice in my blessed hope of glory. Alleluia. Amen."

Wednesday, December 14, 2016

Know that God is present
with you and ready to converse.

"Jesus, you manifested that you are the Christ by many works of mercy. Let your power also work in me."

Read the gospel: Luke 7:18b–23.

John summoned two of his disciples and sent them to the Lord to ask, "Are you the one who is to come, or are we to wait for another?" When the men had come to him, they said, "John the Baptist has sent us to you to ask, 'Are you the one who is to come, or are we to wait for another?'" Jesus had just then cured many people of diseases, plagues, and evil spirits, and had given sight to many who were blind. And he answered them, "Go and tell John what you have seen and heard: the blind receive their sight, the lame walk, the lepers are cleansed, the deaf hear, the dead are raised, the poor have good news brought to them. And blessed is anyone who takes no offence at me."

Notice what you think and feel as you read the gospel.

Without saying so directly, Jesus lets it be known that he is the Christ, the Messiah from God. His works prove it. What he says at the end is intriguing: blessed is the person who takes no offense at him.

Pray as you are led for yourself and others.

"Are you saying that blessed is the one who is not ashamed of you, Lord? Forgive me for the times I have denied you or acted as if I did not know you for fear of what others might think, say, or do . . ." (Continue in your own words.)

Listen to Jesus.

You need not be afraid to own me, beloved, for we are close friends. What else is Jesus saying to you?

Ask God to show you how to live today.

"How may I acknowledge our close friendship before others, Lord? Make me bold by the power of your Spirit. Amen."

Thursday, December 15, 2016

Know that God is present
with you and ready to converse.

"God, you will that I follow Jesus, learning from the
Word of God. Illuminate me."

Read the gospel: Luke 7:24–30.

When John's messengers had gone, Jesus began to
speak to the crowds about John: "What did you go
out into the wilderness to look at? A reed shaken by
the wind? What then did you go out to see? Someone
dressed in soft robes? Look, those who put on fine
clothing and live in luxury are in royal palaces. What
then did you go out to see? A prophet? Yes, I tell you,
and more than a prophet. This is the one about whom
it is written,

> 'See, I am sending my messenger ahead of you,
>   who will prepare your way before you.'

I tell you, among those born of women no one is
greater than John; yet the least in the kingdom of God
is greater than he." (And all the people who heard this,
including the tax-collectors, acknowledged the justice
of God, because they had been baptized with John's
baptism. But by refusing to be baptized by him, the
Pharisees and the lawyers rejected God's purpose for
themselves.)

Notice what you think
and feel as you read the gospel.

Those who believe that John was a prophet and more
than a prophet acknowledge the justice of God for
they had been baptized by him. Those who refused

to be baptized by John rejected God's purpose for themselves.

Pray as you are led for yourself and others.

"God, I do not wish to reject but to accept fully your purpose for me. Soften my heart to obey you. Open my eyes to see your way . . ." (Continue in your own words.)

Listen to Jesus.

Stay with me, dear child, for without me you are in danger. With me you are safe. What else is Jesus saying to you?

Ask God to show you how to live today.

"Great Shepherd, if I am tempted to stray from your path, draw me to yourself. I place my trust in you, my God. Amen."

Friday, December 16, 2016

**Know that God is present
with you and ready to converse.**

"Jesus, you came from the Father. You are coming again at the end of the age. Come to me now."

Read the gospel: John 5:33–36.

Jesus said, "You sent messengers to John, and he testified to the truth. Not that I accept such human testimony, but I say these things so that you may be saved. He was a burning and shining lamp, and you were willing to rejoice for a while in his light. But I have a testimony greater than John's. The works that the Father has given me to complete, the very works that

I am doing, testify on my behalf that the Father has sent me."

Notice what you think and feel as you read the gospel.

Jesus praises John but affirms that he has a testimony greater than John's for he does the very works of the Father who sent him.

Pray as you are led for yourself and others.

"Jesus seems never to doubt his authority, his testimony, his works, or his destiny. He knows who he is, the Son of God sent by the Father. Help me, Lord, to know with certainty who you are and what work you want me to do in your world . . ." (Continue in your own words.)

Listen to Jesus.

By abiding in me, dear disciple, you strengthen the authentic person God made you to be. What else is Jesus saying to you?

Ask God to show you how to live today.

"I want to be the person God wants me to be. Help me stay true to you in everything, today, tomorrow, and always. Thank you, Savior. Amen."

Saturday, December 17, 2016

Know that God is present
with you and ready to converse.

"God is your Father, Lord, yet you took human flesh as a man. I rejoice in your mystery, Son of God and of Son of Man."

Read the gospel: Matthew 1:1–17.

An account of the genealogy of Jesus the Messiah, the son of David, the son of Abraham.

Abraham was the father of Isaac, and Isaac the father of Jacob, and Jacob the father of Judah and his brothers, and Judah the father of Perez and Zerah by Tamar, and Perez the father of Hezron, and Hezron the father of Aram, and Aram the father of Aminadab, and Aminadab the father of Nahshon, and Nahshon the father of Salmon, and Salmon the father of Boaz by Rahab, and Boaz the father of Obed by Ruth, and Obed the father of Jesse, and Jesse the father of King David.

And David was the father of Solomon by the wife of Uriah, and Solomon the father of Rehoboam, and Rehoboam the father of Abijah, and Abijah the father of Asaph, and Asaph the father of Jehoshaphat, and Jehoshaphat the father of Joram, and Joram the father of Uzziah, and Uzziah the father of Jotham, and Jotham the father of Ahaz, and Ahaz the father of Hezekiah, and Hezekiah the father of Manasseh, and Manasseh the father of Amos, and Amos the father of Josiah, and Josiah the father of Jechoniah and his brothers, at the time of the deportation to Babylon.

And after the deportation to Babylon: Jechoniah was the father of Salathiel, and Salathiel the father of Zerubbabel, and Zerubbabel the father of Abiud, and

Abiud the father of Eliakim, and Eliakim the father of
Azor, and Azor the father of Zadok, and Zadok the
father of Achim, and Achim the father of Eliud, and
Eliud the father of Eleazar, and Eleazar the father of
Matthan, and Matthan the father of Jacob, and Jacob
the father of Joseph the husband of Mary, of whom
Jesus was born, who is called the Messiah.

So all the generations from Abraham to David are
fourteen generations; and from David to the deportation to Babylon, fourteen generations; and from
the deportation to Babylon to the Messiah, fourteen
generations.

Notice what you think and feel as you read the gospel.

The Messiah is truly human, a son of Abraham and
part of a long line of people both good and evil, powerful and humble. God's plan in human affairs is inscru-
table and wonderful.

Pray as you are led for yourself and others.

"Your plan for me is also wonderful, Lord. Let me
abandon myself to it. I ask you to lead all those you
have given me along your way . . ." (Continue in your
own words.)

Listen to Jesus.

*Do not be wise in your own eyes, my child. Look to God in
all things.* What else is Jesus saying to you?

Ask God to show you how to live today.

"As I face choices today, Lord, let me discern by your
grace what your way is. Let trust in you grow in my
heart. Amen."

FOURTH WEEK OF ADVENT

Christmas is almost here. As the final touches are being given to the Nativity scene and the Christmas tree—in St. Peter's Square as well—it is necessary to prepare the soul to live intensely this great mystery of faith.

During the final days of Advent, the Liturgy puts particular emphasis on the figure of Mary. The beginning of the Incarnation of the Redeemer took place *in her heart*, from her *"Here I am"* full of faith, in reply to the divine call. If we wish to understand the genuine meaning of Christmas, *we must look at her*, call upon her. Mary, Mother *par excellence*, helps us to understand the key words of the mystery of the birth of her divine Son: *humility, silence, wonder, joy.*

St. John Paul II
December 21, 2003

Sunday, December 18, 2016
Fourth Sunday of Advent

**Know that God is present
with you and ready to converse.**

Almighty God has always been active in human history for God made us in God's image and, though we sinned, seeks to redeem us. God sent the Spirit upon Mary that she might bear God's Son, the Savior. God sent an angel to instruct Joseph, announcing to him that the child shall be named Emmanuel, meaning "God is with us."

"How wonderful are your ways, God. You are with me now."

Read the gospel: Matthew 1:18–24.

Now the birth of Jesus the Messiah took place in this way. When his mother Mary had been engaged to Joseph, but before they lived together, she was found to be with child from the Holy Spirit. Her husband Joseph, being a righteous man and unwilling to expose her to public disgrace, planned to dismiss her quietly. But just when he had resolved to do this, an angel of the Lord appeared to him in a dream and said, "Joseph, son of David, do not be afraid to take Mary as your wife, for the child conceived in her is from the Holy Spirit. She will bear a son, and you are to name him Jesus, for he will save his people from their sins." All this took place to fulfill what had been spoken by the Lord through the prophet:

"Look, the virgin shall conceive and bear a son,
and they shall name him Emmanuel,"

which means, "God is with us." When Joseph awoke from sleep, he did as the angel of the Lord commanded him; he took her as his wife.

Notice what you think and feel as you read the gospel.

This passage focuses on Joseph's response to the pregnancy of Mary. He is a just and reasonable man, and he wants to do what is right, so he plans to dismiss her quietly. But God sends him an angel in a dream to let him know that the pregnancy is of God and that Joseph has a role to play in the coming of the Messiah. Joseph obeys.

Pray as you are led for yourself and others.

"Help me to obey as Joseph obeyed. Make your will clear to me, and give me the grace to do it . . ." (Continue in your own words.)

Listen to Jesus.

I love you. You delight me with your love for me. Ask of me whatever you wish, and I will give you the desires of your heart. What else is Jesus saying to you?

Ask God to show you how to live today.

"You are good to me, Lord. Strengthen my faith, my hope, and especially my love for you and others. Amen."

Monday, December 19, 2016

Know that God is present
with you and ready to converse.

"Constant God of infinite holiness, you work in time
and in the hearts of your people. Prepare me for your
coming, Lord."

Read the gospel: Luke 1:5–25.

In the days of King Herod of Judea, there was a priest
named Zechariah, who belonged to the priestly order
of Abijah. His wife was a descendant of Aaron, and
her name was Elizabeth. Both of them were righteous
before God, living blamelessly according to all the
commandments and regulations of the Lord. But they
had no children, because Elizabeth was barren, and
both were getting on in years.

Once when he was serving as priest before God
and his section was on duty, he was chosen by lot,
according to the custom of the priesthood, to enter the
sanctuary of the Lord and offer incense. Now at the
time of the incense-offering, the whole assembly of the
people was praying outside. Then there appeared to
him an angel of the Lord, standing at the right side of
the altar of incense. When Zechariah saw him, he was
terrified; and fear overwhelmed him. But the angel said
to him, "Do not be afraid, Zechariah, for your prayer
has been heard. Your wife Elizabeth will bear you a
son, and you will name him John. You will have joy
and gladness, and many will rejoice at his birth, for he
will be great in the sight of the Lord. He must never
drink wine or strong drink; even before his birth he
will be filled with the Holy Spirit. He will turn many
of the people of Israel to the Lord their God. With the

spirit and power of Elijah he will go before him, to turn the hearts of parents to their children, and the disobedient to the wisdom of the righteous, to make ready a people prepared for the Lord." Zechariah said to the angel, "How will I know that this is so? For I am an old man, and my wife is getting on in years." The angel replied, "I am Gabriel. I stand in the presence of God, and I have been sent to speak to you and to bring you this good news. But now, because you did not believe my words, which will be fulfilled in their time, you will become mute, unable to speak, until the day these things occur."

Meanwhile, the people were waiting for Zechariah, and wondered at his delay in the sanctuary. When he did come out, he could not speak to them, and they realized that he had seen a vision in the sanctuary. He kept motioning to them and remained unable to speak. When his time of service was ended, he went to his home.

After those days his wife Elizabeth conceived, and for five months she remained in seclusion. She said, "This is what the Lord has done for me when he looked favorably on me and took away the disgrace I have endured among my people."

Notice what you think and feel as you read the gospel.

Because Zechariah cannot believe the announcement of the angel, he is struck mute. Nevertheless, Elizabeth conceives the great prophet John who would come before the Messiah, turning parents toward their children and the disobedient toward the righteous, preparing them for the Lord.

Pray as you are led for yourself and others.

"Lord, turn me in love toward all those you have given me, that I may be ready for you. I long to have you be born in my heart this Advent and Christmas season that I may please you. Dispel my disbelief . . ." (Continue in your own words.)

Listen to Jesus.

As you come to me in prayer, my beloved, I work to prepare you for the kingdom of God. What else is Jesus saying to you?

Ask God to show you how to live today.

"Lord, turn me toward you often. Inspire me to pray. Glory to you, Holy Spirit. Amen."

Tuesday, December 20, 2016

Know that God is present
with you and ready to converse.

"You know my heart, Lord. Let it be open now to your Word."

Read the gospel: Luke 1:26–38.

In the sixth month the angel Gabriel was sent by God to a town in Galilee called Nazareth, to a virgin engaged to a man whose name was Joseph, of the house of David. The virgin's name was Mary. And he came to her and said, "Greetings, favored one! The Lord is with you." But she was much perplexed by his words and pondered what sort of greeting this might be. The angel said to her, "Do not be afraid, Mary, for you have found favor with God. And now, you will conceive in your womb and bear a son, and you will name him Jesus. He will be great, and will be called the Son of the Most High, and the Lord God will give to him the throne of his ancestor David. He will reign over the house of Jacob for ever, and of his kingdom there will be no end." Mary said to the angel, "How can this be, since I am a virgin?" The angel said to her, "The Holy Spirit will come upon you, and the power of the Most High will overshadow you; therefore the child to be born will be holy; he will be called Son of God. And now, your relative Elizabeth in her old age has also conceived a son; and this is the sixth month for her who was said to be barren. For nothing will be impossible with God." Then Mary said, "Here am I, the servant of the Lord; let it be with me according to your word." Then the angel departed from her.

Notice what you think and feel as you read the gospel.

Like Zechariah, Mary doesn't understand how a child can be conceived. Zechariah thought his wife was too old to conceive. Mary is a virgin. But with God all things are possible. Why is Zechariah struck mute for unbelief but Mary suffers nothing? She does say, "let it be with me." Also, God knows her immaculate heart.

Pray as you are led for yourself and others.

"Lord, let me be open to all things that befall me, knowing they come from you. I am your servant, Lord . . ." (Continue in your own words.)

Listen to Jesus.

Hear my voice, servant. I speak to you for your good and the good of those you love. What else is Jesus saying to you?

Ask God to show you how to live today.

"Jesus, let me always hear your voice speaking in my heart. Let me hear you more and more. Amen."

Wednesday, December 21, 2016

**Know that God is present
with you and ready to converse.**

"Lord, your Word is true. Let me believe it in my heart, my soul, my mind. Your Spirit is present with me now."

Read the gospel: Luke 1:39–45.

In those days Mary set out and went with haste to a Judean town in the hill country, where she entered the house of Zechariah and greeted Elizabeth. When Elizabeth heard Mary's greeting, the child leapt in her womb. And Elizabeth was filled with the Holy Spirit and exclaimed with a loud cry, "Blessed are you among women, and blessed is the fruit of your womb. And why has this happened to me, that the mother of my Lord comes to me? For as soon as I heard the sound of your greeting, the child in my womb leapt for joy. And blessed is she who believed that there would be a fulfillment of what was spoken to her by the Lord."

**Notice what you think
and feel as you read the gospel.**

Elizabeth receives her cousin Mary with joy, and the child leaps in her womb. She blesses Mary for her faith, for her great role as the Mother of the Lord. She exclaims at her own good fortune that the Mother of her Lord has come to her.

Pray as you are led for yourself and others.

"Lord, fill me with the expectation of your coming. Fill me with hope. Let me share hope with others . . ." (Continue in your own words.)

Listen to Jesus.

I love you and love to be with you, beloved disciple. Let us walk together in love. What else is Jesus saying to you?

Ask God to show you how to live today.

"Lord, let me turn away from anything in my life that displeases you. Help me to turn fully toward you and your holy will. Thank you. Amen."

Thursday, December 22, 2016

Know that God is present with you and ready to converse.

"Let me magnify you, my Lord, in the same Spirit as your servant Mary."

Read the gospel: Luke 1:46–56.

And Mary said,

"My soul magnifies the Lord,
    and my spirit rejoices in God my Savior,
for he has looked with favor on the lowliness of his
        servant.
    Surely, from now on all generations will call
        me blessed;
for the Mighty One has done great things for me,
    and holy is his name.
His mercy is for those who fear him
    from generation to generation.

He has shown strength with his arm;
>he has scattered the proud in the thoughts of
>>their hearts.
He has brought down the powerful from their
>>thrones,
>and lifted up the lowly;
he has filled the hungry with good things,
>and sent the rich away empty.
He has helped his servant Israel,
>in remembrance of his mercy,
according to the promise he made to our ancestors,
>to Abraham and to his descendants forever."

And Mary remained with her for about three months and then returned to her home.

Notice what you think and feel as you read the gospel.

God scatters the proud and lifts up the lowly, and Mary rejoices because the Lord has looked with favor upon her lowliness. God sends the rich away empty but fills the hungry with good things. God helps his servants and keeps his promises forever.

Pray as you are led for yourself and others.

"Lord, lower me; teach me true humility that I may understand that all I have from you is blessing. I rejoice in you. I pray for those you have given me . . ." (Continue in your own words.)

Listen to Jesus.

You see how it is, my child. Take off all pretense of worthiness and power. Seek God from your lowliness, and you will find God. What else is Jesus saying to you?

Ask God to show you how to live today.

"I live too much in my ego, Lord. Too much is about me. Let me step out of myself today and find you. Let me find you in others. Amen."

Friday, December 23, 2016

**Know that God is present
with you and ready to converse.**

"Open my ears to hear your Word, Lord. Free my tongue to praise you."

Read the gospel: Luke 1:57–66.

Now the time came for Elizabeth to give birth, and she bore a son. Her neighbors and relatives heard that the Lord had shown his great mercy to her, and they rejoiced with her.

On the eighth day they came to circumcise the child, and they were going to name him Zechariah after his father. But his mother said, "No; he is to be called John." They said to her, "None of your relatives has this name." Then they began motioning to his father to find out what name he wanted to give him. He asked for a writing-tablet and wrote, "His name is John." And all of them were amazed. Immediately his mouth was opened and his tongue freed, and he began to speak, praising God. Fear came over all their neighbors, and all these things were talked about throughout the entire hill country of Judea. All who heard them pondered them and said, "What then will this child become?" For, indeed, the hand of the Lord was with him.

Notice what you think
and feel as you read the gospel.

Elizabeth bears a son, and all rejoice. They are skeptical of the name John, however, until mute Zechariah confirms it by writing that name on a tablet. After doing so, his tongue is freed and he praises God. People throughout the hill country of Judea marvel, and they wonder what this child would become.

Pray as you are led for yourself and others.

"Lord, work your purposes in my life and fill me with praise for you. Do great things with me for the glory of your name and the good of others . . ." (Continue in your own words.)

Listen to Jesus.

You are important, beloved disciple. I have work for you. You will serve me in love. What else is Jesus saying to you?

Ask God to show you how to live today.

"I can do only what you give me to do, Lord. I offer all that I am and all that I have to you. Let God be glorified. Amen."

Saturday, December 24, 2016

Know that God is present
with you and ready to converse.

"God, you keep all your promises to your people. I am ready to hear your Word."

Read the gospel: Luke 1:67–79.

Then John's father Zechariah was filled with the Holy Spirit and spoke this prophecy:

"Blessed be the Lord God of Israel,
  for he has looked favorably on his people and
    redeemed them.
He has raised up a mighty savior for us
  in the house of his servant David,
as he spoke through the mouth of his holy prophets
    from of old,
    that we would be saved from our enemies
    and from the hand of all who hate us.
Thus he has shown the mercy promised to our
    ancestors,
  and has remembered his holy covenant,
the oath that he swore to our ancestor Abraham,
  to grant us that we, being rescued from the
    hands of our enemies,
might serve him without fear, in holiness and
    righteousness
  before him all our days.
And you, child, will be called the prophet of the Most
    High;
  for you will go before the Lord to prepare his
    ways,
to give knowledge of salvation to his people
  by the forgiveness of their sins.
By the tender mercy of our God,
  the dawn from on high will break upon us,
to give light to those who sit in darkness and in the
    shadow of death,
  to guide our feet into the way of peace."

Notice what you think and feel as you read the gospel.

Zechariah glorifies God for keeping promises made to his people. Full of the Spirit, he addresses the infant and declares that John will be the prophet of the Most High who prepares the people for the Messiah. The people will have forgiveness of sins, and the dawn shall give light to those who sit in darkness and in the shadow of death.

Pray as you are led for yourself and others.

"Praise to you, O Lord, for you have done what Zechariah prophesied. Guide my feet into the way of your peace . . ." (Continue in your own words.)

Listen to Jesus.

Find your peace in me, beloved. The things that swirl outside and inside need not take away our peace. Share my peace. Love me. What else is Jesus saying to you?

Ask God to show you how to live today.

"Your peace is like no other, Lord. Let me truly be a peaceful person by the power of your Spirit. Let me share that peace with others. Amen."

THE CHRISTMAS SEASON
THROUGH EPIPHANY

Christ is born for us: come, let us adore him!
On this solemn day we come to you,
tender Babe of Bethlehem.
By your birth you have hidden your divinity
in order to share our frail human nature.
In the light of faith, we acknowledge you
as *true* God, *made man* out of love for us.
You alone are the Redeemer of mankind!

St. John Paul II
Christmas, 2004

Sunday, December 25, 2016
Nativity of the Lord

Know that God is present
with you and ready to converse.

Despite the many distractions of the holiday, Christmas is the holy day of the Nativity of our Lord, Jesus Christ. God has come to live with people in the flesh, fully human, yet fully divine. What simplicity and humility to be laid in a manger! What glory did the angels sing!

"Word of God, you became flesh and dwelt among us. Dwell in my heart as I love you."

Read the gospel: John 1:1–18.

In the beginning was the Word, and the Word was with God, and the Word was God. He was in the beginning with God. All things came into being through him, and without him not one thing came into being. What has come into being in him was life, and the life was the light of all people. The light shines in the darkness, and the darkness did not overcome it.

There was a man sent from God, whose name was John. He came as a witness to testify to the light, so that all might believe through him. He himself was not the light, but he came to testify to the light. The true light, which enlightens everyone, was coming into the world.

He was in the world, and the world came into being through him; yet the world did not know him. He came to what was his own, and his own people did not accept him. But to all who received him, who believed in his name, he gave power to become children of God, who were born, not of blood or of the will of the flesh or of the will of man, but of God.

And the Word became flesh and lived among us, and we have seen his glory, the glory as of a father's only son, full of grace and truth. (John testified to him and cried out, "This was he of whom I said, 'He who comes after me ranks ahead of me because he was before me.'") From his fullness we have all received, grace upon grace. The law indeed was given through Moses; grace and truth came through Jesus Christ. No one has ever seen God. It is God the only Son, who is close to the Father's heart, who has made him known.

Notice what you think and feel as you read the gospel.

The eternal Word of God, Jesus Christ, is Life, Light, and God's glory and power to those who accept him as Son of God to become children of God. We are born now not of blood or flesh or the will of humans but of God. All things in the world came into being through this Word—matter, life, and Spirit.

Pray as you are led for yourself and others.

"Most High Triune God, I worship you. I thank you for making me your child. I praise you for . . ." (Continue in your own words.)

Listen to Jesus.

I knew you before you were born, child, and loved you. I will for you to be transformed and come into my kingdom. What else is Jesus saying to you?

Ask God to show you how to live today.

"In the majesty of this mystery, Lord, show me how to live my moments in ways that glorify you and serve others. Walk with me today, my Jesus. Amen."

Monday, December 26, 2016
Saint Stephen, First Martyr

Know that God is present
with you and ready to converse.

"You invite me to follow you even to persecution. I need your grace, Lord."

Read the gospel: Matthew 10:17–22.

Jesus taught his disciples, "Beware of them, for they will hand you over to councils and flog you in their synagogues; and you will be dragged before governors and kings because of me, as a testimony to them and the Gentiles. When they hand you over, do not worry about how you are to speak or what you are to say; for what you are to say will be given to you at that time; for it is not you who speak, but the Spirit of your Father speaking through you. Brother will betray brother to death, and a father his child, and children will rise against parents and have them put to death; and you will be hated by all because of my name. But the one who endures to the end will be saved."

Notice what you think
and feel as you read the gospel.

Jesus wants his disciples to endure betrayals and persecutions to the end so he warns them of some of the terrible things that will befall them—floggings, trials, accusations, betrayals, hatred—because of his name. We see how it worked out for the first martyr of the Church, St. Stephen, legions of martyrs through history, and many even in our day. When persecuted, we can rely on Jesus' promise of the Spirit with us. We can rest in the Spirit.

Pray as you are led for yourself and others.

"This warning is frightening, but why should a follower of the Crucified have a different path than the sinless Lord? Let me accept persecution for your name and rely on the Spirit. I pray for the persecuted today . . ." (Continue in your own words.)

Listen to Jesus.

I am with you always, beloved disciple. Rely on me and on my Spirit for words, for grace, and for endurance. What else is Jesus saying to you?

Ask God to show you how to live today.

"Remind me to forgive and to pray for anyone who opposes me, even in the smallest way. Help me follow you, Jesus. Amen."

Tuesday, December 27, 2016
Saint John, Apostle and Evangelist

Know that God is present with you and ready to converse.

"Risen Lord, I run to you now. Let me see and believe your Word."

Read the gospel: John 20:1–8.

Early on the first day of the week, while it was still dark, Mary Magdalene came to the tomb and saw that the stone had been removed from the tomb. So she ran and went to Simon Peter and the other disciple, the one whom Jesus loved, and said to them, "They have taken the Lord out of the tomb, and we do not know where they have laid him." Then Peter and the other disciple set out and went towards the tomb. The two were running together, but the other disciple outran Peter and reached the tomb first. He bent down to look in and saw the linen wrappings lying there, but he did not go in. Then Simon Peter came, following him, and went into the tomb. He saw the linen wrappings lying there, and the cloth that had been on Jesus' head, not lying with the linen wrappings but rolled up in a place by itself. Then the other disciple, who reached the tomb first, also went in, and he saw and believed.

Notice what you think
and feel as you read the gospel.

After Jesus' resurrection, the story turns to how the disciples came to know of it and understand it. St. John's gospel begins with a woman who in the dark sees that the stone has been removed from the tomb. She runs to tell Peter and John who themselves run to the tomb. John arrives first and hesitates, but Peter rushes in. He sees the linen wrappings lying there and the head cloth rolled up separately. Then John goes in, sees what Peter sees, and believes. The story will continue from here.

Pray as you are led for yourself and others.

"What did Peter and John believe, Lord? I ask for that faith that I, too, may serve you as they did in my life and in my death . . ." (Continue in your own words.)

Listen to Jesus.

You are my beloved disciple, for you love me only as you can. What else is Jesus saying to you?

Ask God to show you how to live today.

"I do love you, Lord. Magnify this love in me so that I may please you more and more. Let me show our love to others. Amen."

Wednesday, December 28, 2016
Holy Innocents, Martyrs

**Know that God is present
with you and ready to converse.**

"Lord, I cling to you. You are my light and my salvation."

Read the gospel: Matthew 2:13–18.

Now after the magi had left, an angel of the Lord appeared to Joseph in a dream and said, "Get up, take the child and his mother, and flee to Egypt, and remain there until I tell you; for Herod is about to search for the child, to destroy him." Then Joseph got up, took the child and his mother by night, and went to Egypt, and remained there until the death of Herod. This was to fulfill what had been spoken by the Lord through the prophet, "Out of Egypt I have called my son."

When Herod saw that he had been tricked by the wise men, he was infuriated, and he sent and killed all the children in and around Bethlehem who were two years old or under, according to the time that he had learned from the wise men. Then was fulfilled what had been spoken through the prophet Jeremiah:

"A voice was heard in Ramah,
    wailing and loud lamentation,
Rachel weeping for her children;
    she refused to be consoled, because they are
        no more."

Notice what you think and feel as you read the gospel.

The angel warns Joseph to escape the cruelty of Herod, so the Holy Family flees to Egypt. Meanwhile, Herod is furious to have been tricked by the wise men. He kills all the children younger than two years of age in and around Bethlehem, fulfilling Jeremiah's doleful prophesy of wailing and loud lamentation for the children are no more.

Pray as you are led for yourself and others.

"As I grieve for the atrocities committed in my own time, Lord, let me trust that somehow your will will be done, even in the aftermath of evil . . ." (Continue in your own words.)

Listen to Jesus.

In this age, God allows evil to continue. But justice will prevail. I have overcome the world. Child, apply yourself to doing good. What else is Jesus saying to you?

Ask God to show you how to live today.
"By your grace, Lord, I will persevere in doing good, seeking peace, and working for justice for all. Amen."

Thursday, December 29, 2016

Know that God is present
with you and ready to converse.
"Let your Word be a light of revelation in my heart, mind, and soul, mighty God."

Read the gospel: Luke 2:22–35.
When the time came for their purification according to the law of Moses, they brought him up to Jerusalem to present him to the Lord (as it is written in the law of the Lord, "Every firstborn male shall be designated as holy to the Lord"), and they offered a sacrifice according to what is stated in the law of the Lord, "a pair of turtle-doves or two young pigeons."

Now there was a man in Jerusalem whose name was Simeon; this man was righteous and devout, looking forward to the consolation of Israel, and the Holy Spirit rested on him. It had been revealed to him by the Holy Spirit that he would not see death before he had seen the Lord's Messiah. Guided by the Spirit, Simeon came into the temple; and when the parents brought in the child Jesus, to do for him what was customary under the law, Simeon took him in his arms and praised God, saying,

"Master, now you are dismissing your servant in
peace,
according to your word;
for my eyes have seen your salvation,

which you have prepared in the presence of
     all peoples,
a light for revelation to the Gentiles
     and for glory to your people Israel."

And the child's father and mother were amazed at
what was being said about him. Then Simeon blessed
them and said to his mother Mary, "This child is destined for the falling and the rising of many in Israel,
and to be a sign that will be opposed so that the inner
thoughts of many will be revealed—and a sword will
pierce your own soul too."

Notice what you think and feel as you read the gospel.

Obedient to the law, Joseph and Mary present the
infant Jesus to aged Simeon in the temple. God had
revealed to Simeon that he would not die before he had
seen the Messiah. When Simeon saw Jesus he praised
God for he knew he was holding in his arms the salvation of the world. After blessing them, Simeon spoke of
the opposition the child would evoke in Israel, saying
a sword would pierce Mary's soul, too.

Pray as you are led for yourself and others.

"I share the amazement of Joseph and Mary, Lord. Let
all things happen as you have ordained, for you are
great and good . . ." (Continue in your own words.)

Listen to Jesus.

*There is a sword and a cross for all who follow me, dear
one. Find comfort in my Holy Spirit.* What else is Jesus
saying to you?

Ask God to show you how to live today.

"With you, Lord, I can do anything, suffer anything. Let your glory be revealed. I praise you. Amen."

Friday, December 30, 2016
Holy Family of Jesus, Mary, and Joseph

**Know that God is present
with you and ready to converse.**

"As you guided the Holy Family, Lord, guide me in my life by your Word."

Read the gospel: Matthew 2:13–15, 19–23.

Now after they had left, an angel of the Lord appeared to Joseph in a dream and said, "Get up, take the child and his mother, and flee to Egypt, and remain there until I tell you; for Herod is about to search for the child, to destroy him." Then Joseph got up, took the child and his mother by night, and went to Egypt, and remained there until the death of Herod. This was to fulfill what had been spoken by the Lord through the prophet, "Out of Egypt I have called my son." . . .

When Herod died, an angel of the Lord suddenly appeared in a dream to Joseph in Egypt and said, "Get up, take the child and his mother, and go to the land of Israel, for those who were seeking the child's life are dead." Then Joseph got up, took the child and his mother, and went to the land of Israel. But when he heard that Archelaus was ruling over Judea in place of his father Herod, he was afraid to go there. And after being warned in a dream, he went away to the district of Galilee. There he made his home in a town called Nazareth, so that what had been spoken through the prophets might be fulfilled, "He will be called a Nazorean."

Notice what you think
and feel as you read the gospel.

Joseph was an active dreamer in those days. In his sleep, angels speak to him, directing him to Egypt to escape Herod and then back to Israel but to another place there, the town Nazareth in Galilee—all this in fulfillment of the words of the prophets.

Pray as you are led for yourself and others.

"Let me trust you are also guiding me, Lord. Let your Word be fulfilled in me and in those I pray for . . ." (Continue in your own words.)

Listen to Jesus.

I do guide you for you are a child in this holy family. Have no fear. What else is Jesus saying to you?

Ask God to show you how to live today.

"I wish to grow in wisdom and in grace that I may be an honor to this holy family of God. You will grant me what I ask, Lord. Amen."

Saturday, December 31, 2016

Know that God is present
with you and ready to converse.

"Most High Lord of Hosts, your Word is infinite. Let it swell my mind to grasp it and my heart to love and obey it."

Read the gospel: John 1:1–18.

In the beginning was the Word, and the Word was with God, and the Word was God. He was in the beginning with God. All things came into being through him, and without him not one thing came into being. What has come into being in him was life, and the life was the light of all people. The light shines in the darkness, and the darkness did not overcome it.

There was a man sent from God, whose name was John. He came as a witness to testify to the light, so that all might believe through him. He himself was not the light, but he came to testify to the light. The true light, which enlightens everyone, was coming into the world.

He was in the world, and the world came into being through him; yet the world did not know him. He came to what was his own, and his own people did not accept him. But to all who received him, who believed in his name, he gave power to become children of God, who were born, not of blood or of the will of the flesh or of the will of man, but of God.

And the Word became flesh and lived among us, and we have seen his glory, the glory as of a father's only son, full of grace and truth. (John testified to him and cried out, "This was he of whom I said, 'He who comes after me ranks ahead of me because he was before me.'") From his fullness we have all received, grace upon grace. The law indeed was given through Moses; grace and truth came through Jesus Christ. No one has ever seen God. It is God the only Son, who is close to the Father's heart, who has made him known.

Notice what you think and feel as you read the gospel.

Although God created all things, the world is shrouded in darkness because of sin. God, out of love for sinners, sends the Light into the world, and the darkness does not overcome it. The Light shines on the whole world, but the world does not know it, does not accept him, the Word of God, the Son of God. But those who do accept him receive grace upon grace.

Pray as you are led for yourself and others.

"Lord, I, too, walk among the darkness—even darkness within me. Be my light. Be a light unto others, especially those you have given me . . ." (Continue in your own words.)

Listen to Jesus.

The glory of God is being revealed in you, beloved. Enter into the love between us. What else is Jesus saying to you?

Ask God to show you how to live today.

"I have the treasure of your grace in an earthen vessel, Lord. Make me more and more a temple of your Spirit. Amen."

Sunday, January 1, 2017
Blessed Virgin Mary,
the Holy Mother of God

Know that God is present
with you and ready to converse.

Mary has given birth to her child and named him Jesus as instructed by the angel. Now they remain in that humble place outside of Bethlehem, a stable. The child lies in a manger. Now come the shepherds with amazing news Mary would ponder all her life.

"Sweet Child of God, I come with the shepherds to adore you and praise you."

Read the gospel: Luke 2:16–21.

So the shepherds went with haste and found Mary and Joseph, and the child lying in the manger. When they saw this, they made known what had been told them about this child; and all who heard it were amazed at what the shepherds told them. But Mary treasured all these words and pondered them in her heart. The shepherds returned, glorifying and praising God for all they had heard and seen, as it had been told them.

After eight days had passed, it was time to circumcise the child; and he was called Jesus, the name given by the angel before he was conceived in the womb.

Notice what you think
and feel as you read the gospel.

After being directed by an angel and having witnessed the heavenly host praising God, the shepherds find Mary, Joseph, and the infant in the manger. The shepherds tell Mary and Joseph what they had heard from the angel about this child, and Mary treasures their words and ponders them in her heart. The shepherds return to their fields, rejoicing in God.

Pray as you are led for yourself and others.

"I rejoice in the trustworthiness of the Word of God. I praise the works of God in history and in my life . . ." (Continue in your own words.)

Listen to Jesus.

I am the same yesterday, today, and forever, dear one. Ask me for whatever you want today. What else is Jesus saying to you?

Ask God to show you how to live today.

"Help me stay very close to you every moment of this day. Let me practice your presence in all I think, do, and say. Amen."

Monday, January 2, 2017

Know that God is present with you and ready to converse.

"You are with me now, Lord. Let me know you in your Word."

Read the gospel: John 1:19–28.

This is the testimony given by John when the Jews sent priests and Levites from Jerusalem to ask him, "Who are you?" He confessed and did not deny it, but confessed, "I am not the Messiah." And they asked him, "What then? Are you Elijah?" He said, "I am not." "Are you the prophet?" He answered, "No." Then they said to him, "Who are you? Let us have an answer for

those who sent us. What do you say about yourself?"
He said,

"I am the voice of one crying out in the wilderness,
'Make straight the way of the Lord,'"

as the prophet Isaiah said.

Now they had been sent from the Pharisees. They asked him, "Why then are you baptizing if you are neither the Messiah, nor Elijah, nor the prophet?" John answered them, "I baptize with water. Among you stands one whom you do not know, the one who is coming after me; I am not worthy to untie the thong of his sandal." This took place in Bethany across the Jordan where John was baptizing.

Notice what you think and feel as you read the gospel.

John the Baptist is interrogated by the priests and Levites. They want to know just who he is. He answers them with scripture from Isaiah that he is the voice crying in the wilderness to make straight the way of the Lord. He goes on to tell them that one stands among them who they do not know, the one who is coming after him whose sandal he is not worthy to untie. Were they happy, puzzled, or dismayed to hear this?

Pray as you are led for yourself and others.

"God, I do not want to miss my moment to know you and love you. Baptize me with your Spirit and . . ." (Continue in your own words.)

Listen to Jesus.

I rejoice in your love, child of God. Follow me and all will be well with you. What else is Jesus saying to you?

Ask God to show you how to live today.

"You are good to me, Lord. Show me how to be good to others today. Glory to God in the highest. Amen."

Tuesday, January 3, 2017

**Know that God is present
with you and ready to converse.**

"Let me receive the testimony of the prophets, Lord, for they speak what they know."

Read the gospel: John 1:29–34.

The next day John saw Jesus coming towards him and declared, "Here is the Lamb of God who takes away the sin of the world! This is he of whom I said, 'After me comes a man who ranks ahead of me because he was before me.' I myself did not know him; but I came baptizing with water for this reason, that he might be revealed to Israel." And John testified, "I saw the Spirit descending from heaven like a dove, and it remained on him. I myself did not know him, but the one who sent me to baptize with water said to me, 'He on whom you see the Spirit descend and remain is the one who baptizes with the Holy Spirit.' And I myself have seen and have testified that this is the Son of God."

**Notice what you think
and feel as you read the gospel.**

John recognizes Jesus as the Lamb of God who takes away the sins of the world. Does he know that Jesus is destined to be a sacrificial lamb? He certainly knows Jesus ranks ahead of him and existed before him. Does he know that Jesus is one with God? He testifies that Jesus is the Son of God because he saw the Spirit descend and remain on him.

Pray as you are led for yourself and others.

"Lamb of God, take away my sins and baptize me with the Holy Spirit that I may please you always . . ." (Continue in your own words.)

Listen to Jesus.

I take away your sins and baptize you, dear disciple. Give my gifts to others. What else is Jesus saying to you?

Ask God to show you how to live today.

"Guide me in my giving, doing, and praying today, Lord. Let me give as generously as I have received. Thank you for taking away my sins, Lamb of God. Amen."

Wednesday, January 4, 2017

Know that God is present with you and ready to converse.

"I come into your presence with awe, Lord, for you are the living God who sustains the whole universe by your Word."

Read the gospel: John 1:35–42.

The next day John again was standing with two of his disciples, and as he watched Jesus walk by, he exclaimed, "Look, here is the Lamb of God!" The two disciples heard him say this, and they followed Jesus. When Jesus turned and saw them following, he said to them, "What are you looking for?" They said to him, "Rabbi" (which translated means Teacher), "where are you staying?" He said to them, "Come and see." They came and saw where he was staying, and they remained with him that day. It was about four o'clock in the afternoon. One of the two who heard John speak and followed him was Andrew, Simon Peter's brother. He first found his brother Simon and said to him, "We have found the Messiah" (which is translated Anointed). He brought Simon to Jesus, who looked at him and said, "You are Simon son of John. You are to be called Cephas" (which is translated Peter).

Notice what you think and feel as you read the gospel.

Jesus' first disciples are drawn to him by the words of John the Baptist. He does not recruit them, but he invites them to come and see where he is staying. Andrew tells his brother Simon that they have found the Messiah. When Simon comes to see him, Jesus identifies him as Cephas, Peter.

Pray as you are led for yourself and others.

"Lord, let me come and see you. Please know me as your own and let me be a true disciple that others may also come to you . . ." (Continue in your own words.)

Listen to Jesus.

Those who follow me must forsake worldly desires. They must set their hearts on God. Are you ready for that? What else is Jesus saying to you?

Ask God to show you how to live today.

"Only by your grace can I aspire to and do your will, Lord. Fill me and make me new. Amen."

Thursday, January 5, 2017

**Know that God is present
with you and ready to converse.**

"I desire to see you in all things, Lord, but especially in your Word here and now."

Read the gospel: John 1:43–51.

The next day Jesus decided to go to Galilee. He found Philip and said to him, "Follow me." Now Philip was from Bethsaida, the city of Andrew and Peter. Philip found Nathanael and said to him, "We have found him about whom Moses in the law and also the prophets wrote, Jesus son of Joseph from Nazareth." Nathanael said to him, "Can anything good come out of Nazareth?" Philip said to him, "Come and see." When Jesus saw Nathanael coming towards him, he said of him, "Here is truly an Israelite in whom there is no deceit!" Nathanael asked him, "Where did you come to know me?" Jesus answered, "I saw you under the fig tree before Philip called you." Nathanael replied, "Rabbi, you are the Son of God! You are the King of Israel!" Jesus answered, "Do you believe because I told you that I saw you under the fig tree? You will see greater things than these." And he said to him, "Very truly, I tell you, you will see heaven opened and the angels of God ascending and descending upon the Son of Man."

**Notice what you think
and feel as you read the gospel.**

Jesus knows Nathanael inside and out, amazing Nathanael and prompting him to believe that Jesus is the Son of God. Jesus tells him he hasn't seen anything yet. Nathanael will see heaven open one day and the angels ascending and descending upon Jesus.

Pray as you are led for yourself and others.

"Lord, let me be a person in whom there is no deceit. Let me be honest with you and with all whom I encounter. Let me be honest with myself. . . ." (Continue in your own words.)

Listen to Jesus.

I am the Truth, beloved disciple. Cling to me, and you will be part of the great truth of God. What else is Jesus saying to you?

Ask God to show you how to live today.

"Open my eyes to your presence, Lord, especially in those people, situations, and things I might otherwise not see. Thank you. Amen."

Friday, January 6, 2017

Know that God is present
with you and ready to converse.

"Lord, you are Spirit and Father of the Word, your beloved Son."

Read the gospel: Mark 1:7–11.

John proclaimed, "The one who is more powerful than I is coming after me; I am not worthy to stoop down and untie the thong of his sandals. I have baptized you with water; but he will baptize you with the Holy Spirit."

In those days Jesus came from Nazareth of Galilee and was baptized by John in the Jordan. And just as he was coming up out of the water, he saw the heavens torn apart and the Spirit descending like a dove on him. And a voice came from heaven, "You are my Son, the Beloved; with you I am well pleased."

Notice what you think and feel as you read the gospel.

John the Baptist proclaims that the great one who is coming after him will baptize not with water but with the Holy Spirit. The Spirit descends from above on Jesus when he is baptized by John, and the voice from heaven calls Jesus "my Son, the Beloved."

Pray as you are led for yourself and others.

"What a moment that must have been, Lord! God was present as Jesus began his earthly ministry. Be present with me, Spirit of God . . ." (Continue in your own words.)

Listen to Jesus.

Allow me to lead you, dear follower. Give yourself to me. I care for you. What else is Jesus saying to you?

Ask God to show you how to live today.

"I want to love you better, Jesus, and walk more closely with you. How may I please you today? Amen."

Saturday, January 7, 2017

Know that God is present with you and ready to converse.

"Lord, reveal your glory to me. I turn to your Word for light and life."

Read the gospel: John 2:1–11.

On the third day there was a wedding in Cana of Galilee, and the mother of Jesus was there. Jesus and his disciples had also been invited to the wedding. When the wine gave out, the mother of Jesus said to him, "They have no wine." And Jesus said to her, "Woman, what concern is that to you and to me? My hour has not yet come." His mother said to the servants, "Do whatever he tells you." Now standing there were six stone water-jars for the Jewish rites of purification, each holding twenty or thirty gallons. Jesus said to them, "Fill the jars with water." And they filled them up to the brim. He said to them, "Now draw some out, and take it to the chief steward." So they took it. When the steward tasted the water that had become wine, and did not know where it came from (though the servants who had drawn the water knew), the steward called the bridegroom and said to him, "Everyone serves the good wine first, and then the inferior wine after the guests have become drunk. But you have kept the good wine until now." Jesus did this, the first of his signs, in Cana of Galilee, and revealed his glory; and his disciples believed in him.

Notice what you think and feel as you read the gospel.

Jesus performs his first sign at a wedding. It is a simple, practical, yet extravagant sign for he changes much water into good wine. He refers to himself as the Bridegroom throughout his ministry. He loves his bride and lays down his life for her, for us.

Pray as you are led for yourself and others.

"Redeemer, you have power to transform elements. Transform me. Let me drink the wine of your Blood that I may be one with you . . ." (Continue in your own words.)

Listen to Jesus.

Come and drink my cup, beloved. It is eternal life. What else is Jesus saying to you?

Ask God to show you how to live today.

"Let me be full of awe at the mysteries of your words, your life, your death, and your resurrection. Lord, I glorify you and give you thanks for your great glory. Amen."

Sunday, January 8, 2017
Epiphany of the Lord

**Know that God is present
with you and ready to converse.**

Mary has her baby. Born of God and Mary, he is Emmanuel, "God is with us." Immediately, God begins to reveal the Son who is destined to become king, a ruler to shepherd God's people. Overjoyed, the wise men find him in Bethlehem and kneel before the baby.

"Let me come and worship, too, Lord. Here is my heart."

Read the gospel: Matthew 2:1–12.

In the time of King Herod, after Jesus was born in Bethlehem of Judea, wise men from the East came to

Jerusalem, asking, "Where is the child who has been born king of the Jews? For we observed his star at its rising, and have come to pay him homage." When King Herod heard this, he was frightened, and all Jerusalem with him; and calling together all the chief priests and scribes of the people, he inquired of them where the Messiah was to be born. They told him, "In Bethlehem of Judea; for so it has been written by the prophet:

'And you, Bethlehem, in the land of Judah,
    are by no means least among the rulers of
        Judah;
for from you shall come a ruler
    who is to shepherd my people Israel.'"

Then Herod secretly called for the wise men and learned from them the exact time when the star had appeared. Then he sent them to Bethlehem, saying, "Go and search diligently for the child; and when you have found him, bring me word so that I may also go and pay him homage." When they had heard the king, they set out; and there, ahead of them, went the star that they had seen at its rising, until it stopped over the place where the child was. When they saw that the star had stopped, they were overwhelmed with joy. On entering the house, they saw the child with Mary his mother; and they knelt down and paid him homage. Then, opening their treasure-chests, they offered him gifts of gold, frankincense, and myrrh. And having been warned in a dream not to return to Herod, they left for their own country by another road.

Notice what you think and feel as you read the gospel.

Ironically, the mysterious wise men learn the infant Messiah's location from Herod, the chief priests, and the scribes—all of whom would sooner or later seek to kill Jesus. God also guides them by the star to the place and later by a dream so they do not return to Herod.

Pray as you are led for yourself and others.

"Guide me to you, Lord, and guide those I love to you. Guide all those you have given me to you . . ." (Continue in your own words.)

Listen to Jesus.

I came to shepherd my people, and I will always do so. You have entrusted yourself to me, beloved, and I am trust-worthy. What else is Jesus saying to you?

Ask God to show you how to live today.

"I would like others to recognize you as the Great Shepherd. Open the eyes and hearts of those who are closed to you. Let me know what I may do to help. Amen."

Please Take Our Survey!
Now that you've finished reading *Sacred Reading for Advent and Christmas 2016–2017*, please go to **avemariapress.com/feedback** to take a brief survey about your experience. Ave Maria Press and the Apostleship of Prayer appreciate your feedback.

The Apostleship of Prayer is an international Jesuit prayer ministry that reaches more than 35 million members worldwide through its popular website, apostleshipofprayer.org, and through talks, conferences, publications, and retreats. Known as "the pope's worldwide prayer network," the Apostleship's mission is to encourage Christians to make a daily offering of themselves to the Lord in union with the Sacred Heart of Jesus.

Douglas Leonard is executive director of the Apostleship of Prayer in the United States, where he has served since 2006. He earned a bachelor's degree in English in 1976, a master's degree in English in 1977, and a PhD in English in 1981, all from the University of Wisconsin-Madison. Leonard also has served in higher education, professional development, publishing, and instructional design as an executive, writer, editor, educator, and consultant.